D1542461

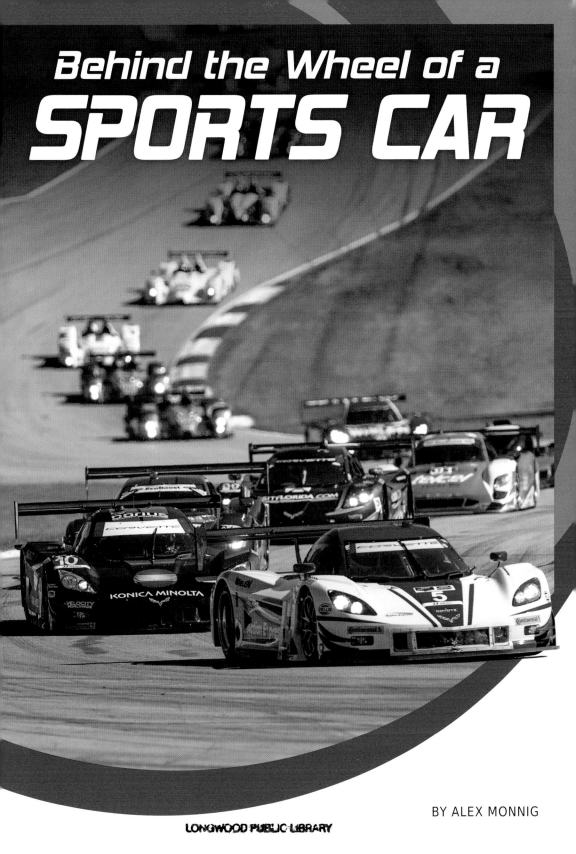

Behind the Wheel of a
SPORTS CAR

BY ALEX MONNIG

Published by The Child's World®
1980 Lookout Drive • Mankato, MN 56003-1705
800-599-READ • www.childsworld.com

Acknowledgments
The Child's World®: Mary Berendes, Publishing Director
Red Line Editorial: Design, editorial direction, and production
Photographs ©: Andrew Snook/Icon Sportswire/AP Images, cover, 1;
Shutterstock Images, 4; Regis Duvignau/Reuters/Corbis, 7; iStockphoto, 8,
10; Eric Preau/Sygma/Corbis, 12; Rainier Ehrhardt/AP Images/Corbis, 15;
David Merrett CC2.0, 16, 18; Oskar Schuler/Shutterstock Images, 21

ISBN 9781634074322

LCCN 2015946271

Printed in the United States of America
Mankato, MN
December, 2015
PA02282

Table of
CONTENTS

Chapter 1

A TEST OF ENDURANCE

You feel unstoppable. You are gliding around the track in your team's shiny silver sports car. It is sleek and stylish. Its handling makes it easy to **hug** the corners of the track. You are on your third straight hour of **endurance** racing.

You grew up watching stock car and Indy car races. Those races usually lasted a few hours. But one day you met a new kid in school. He had moved to your hometown from Europe. He told you about endurance racing. He said the races were longer. Some lasted up to 24 hours. You could not imagine how drivers did it. You wanted to learn everything about the racing strategies.

So you did. And now, years later, you find yourself in the middle of huge race. It is the 24 Hours of Le Mans, a race in France. You and your team are trying to win your first major competition.

◀ **Unlike Indy cars, sports cars must have covered wheels and two seats.**

The key is to balance speed with technique. You want to cover as many miles as possible in 24 hours. But you do not want your car to break down. You and the other drivers take turns racing the car. You are often tearing down the track at more than 100 mph (161 km/h). Your team is constantly trying to plan ahead.

But some things you cannot plan for. You are half a lap away from your team's pit area. It is almost time to change drivers. You need to get around two cars in front of you. One is cherry red and one is black. You speed up. The red car tries to speed ahead to take a turn. But the black car does not want to allow it past. That driver also speeds up.

The two cars bump each other and start to spin out of control. They are only a few feet in front of you. You see the race flash before your eyes. All the time you spent practicing. The hours of working on the car. All the laps your team has already completed today.

It all might be wasted in a few seconds. Even worse, you and your opponents could get seriously injured. As the uncontrolled cars get closer, you have moments to avoid disaster.

When there is a crash on the track, a pace car leads racers ▶ slowly around the track until the debris is cleaned up.

Chapter 2

WHAT IS A SPORTS CAR?

You grew up seeing sports cars off the track. They were common on the roads and highways around your hometown. You knew that companies made popular sports cars for people to buy. But you learned from your new classmate that racing sports cars was very different.

You found out that competition sports cars are similar in some ways to race cars, such as Indy cars and stock cars. But sports cars also have many unique features. This is because the races are very different. Indy and stock cars are built mostly for speed. They race for a certain number of laps. Whichever driver finishes the laps the quickest wins the race. But sports cars need to be built for endurance.

Your classmate's favorite sports cars were Grand Touring (GT) cars. These are popular in Europe. In fact, the name comes from

◄ Unlike most other auto races, sports car endurance races can last through the night.

the Italian term *Gran Turismo*. GT cars became popular in the early 1900s. They helped inspire modern sports cars.

You always loved the way sports cars looked. But the idea that some sports cars were made for long races made you more interested. You started reading more about sports car racing. You learned there are three main classes of sports cars. They race in the World Endurance Championship, the main racing circuit. The classes are Le Mans Prototype 1 (LMP 1), Le Mans Prototype 2 (LMP 2), and Le Mans Grand Touring Endurance (LM GTE).

Big car companies make LMP 1 cars. Manufacturers often experiment with LMP 1 cars. They try new technology and use the most advanced parts on the cars. Private teams make LMP 2 cars. They are similar to LMP 1 cars. But private teams often run on much smaller budgets.

The LMP 1 and LMP 2 cars look very different from regular cars. They are flatter. They have a small seating area for the driver. LM GTE cars look more like regular cars. They can be driven on the open road. Non-racers can purchase them. They have two doors. They also have two front seats and sometimes two back seats.

◀ **LMP 2 cars often sit low to the ground and have smooth curves to help them cut through the air.**

Chapter 3

HOW A RACE WORKS

Y ou talked to your new European friend about sports car racing whenever you could. You still had a lot of questions. Luckily for you, your classmate loved discussing it.

He helped you understand endurance racing. It was a lot different than other motorsports you had seen on TV. In most motorsports competitions, drivers try to get around a track a certain number of times as fast as possible. Whichever driver crosses the finish line first wins.

Endurance races take the opposite approach. Instead of measuring how quickly a car can travel a set distance, sports car races measured how far a car can travel in a given time period. Whichever car covers the most distance in that time wins.

◄ **Thousands of people gather at the start of the 24 Hours of Le Mans.**

FUEL RESTRICTIONS AT LE MANS

The 24 Hours of Le Mans might be the most famous endurance race. Officials added a new wrinkle to the race in 2014. They put a limit on how much fuel cars can use. It is measured every three laps. Teams put computerized limits on the cars. Sometimes cars are on pace to go over the limit. Driving faster uses more fuel, so the cars automatically slow down to save fuel.

Your friend had been to the 24 Hours of Le Mans. He told you about the experience. Hundreds of thousands of people come to watch the race. The track is a mixture of racetrack and normal roads.

Because the race is so long, teams switch drivers every couple of hours. The drivers eat and rest between driving shifts. Without these breaks, they would not be able to focus as much as they need to. This would be bad for a team trying to win the race. More importantly, it would be dangerous.

Teams at Le Mans are allowed to use three drivers each. They take turns behind the wheel. That means racing teams' strategies

In long races, drivers take turns driving a single car. ▶
They switch during pit stops.

are super important. The race requires speed for success. But it is impossible to keep the pedal to the metal the whole time. Teams need to figure out the best time to switch drivers. This becomes even harder when the rules limit the amount of fuel cars can use.

Your friend told you some drivers used to try to finish endurance races on their own. But major races made rules to protect drivers. They restrict drivers to a certain amount of time behind the wheel. This includes hours in a row as well as total hours raced. The races also require each car to be driven by a minimum number of people during the race.

Learning about sports car races made you want to get involved. You volunteered with a small local team while you were still in school. It changed your life. You have been involved with sports cars ever since. Eventually, you moved from the pit into the driver's seat.

◄ LM GTE races use cars that are mass-produced. This makes the races more accessible to teams that are just starting out.

Chapter 4

RACING AROUND THE WORLD

Learning to drive a sports car took years of training. Just getting used to the car was hard enough. But building up your **stamina** was also difficult. You did not expect to find it so tough. Being able to stay focused on the race for hours at a time is what separates the best drivers from all others.

You started racing in small races. You and your team got better and better as the years passed. Your pit stops became quicker. You agreed about when to switch drivers and when to stop for new tires.

The longer the race, the better you finished. Eventually, a large car company became interested. They wanted to **sponsor** you. They hired you and your whole team to represent them at the highest level.

◀ Crews take the coverings off LMP 1 cars before races to make sure everything is ready to race.

Today, you race in the World Endurance Championship. The series brings you to races around the globe. It started in 2012. It is run by the Fédération Internationale de l'Automobile. This organization makes up the standard rules of sports car racing. Before the World Endurance Championship, there was the World Sports Car Championship. It ran from 1953 to 1992.

TRIPLE CROWN RACING

Many consider three races to be the most important sports car races. They are the 24 Hours of Le Mans, the Rolex 24 at Daytona, and the 12 Hours of Sebring. These three races form the Triple Crown of endurance racing. It is not an official title. But it is well respected in the world of racing. Several drivers have won all three.

Today's World Endurance Championship features the best teams in the world.

Your opponents represent car companies, such as Audi, Porsche, and Toyota. Dozens of teams enter each year. Your goal is to finish in the top of the standings to win your team points. The team with the most total points at the end of the circuit wins.

It has been a long season and a long race. You are a few hundred feet away from a rest. Your arms are tired. Your brain is frazzled.

▲ During pit stops, teams switch drivers, replace tires, refuel, and fix issues with the car.

You need to recover. But the spinning red and black cars have jolted you back to reality.

You know you cannot slam on the brakes. That would cause you to lose control. You remember your training. You stay calm. You see the cars spinning. They are headed off the track. As soon as you can, you hit the gas. You fly by, untouched. That was close.

You pull over to your team's pit area. There is no time to relax. You hop out of the car as fast as possible. Your teammate hops in and is off before you know it. Time to recover. In a few hours, you have another four hours of racing ahead of you.

GLOSSARY

circuit (SUR-kit): A circuit is a series of races. The World Endurance Championship is the biggest circuit in endurance racing.

classes (klas-iz): Classes are certain levels of racing. There are three main classes of sports car racing.

endurance (en-DOOR-uhns): Endurance racing involves races that can last up to 24 hours. The 24 Hours of Le Mans is maybe the most famous endurance race.

hug (huhg): In racing, to hug is to stay close to. Racers hug turns tightly to make it around the track as fast as possible.

laps (laps): The number of laps is equal to the number of times a car goes around the track. You try to complete as many laps as possible in the allotted time during endurance races.

pit area (pit AIR-ee-uh): The pit area is the place in which you take your car for quick breaks during races. You needed to get around the spinning cars to get to the pit area.

sponsor (SPON-ser): To sponsor is to pay for racing costs. Big car companies sponsor sports car drivers in races.

stamina (STAM-uh-nuh): Stamina is being able to continue doing something for a long time. Driving in endurance races requires a lot of stamina.

TO LEARN MORE

Books

Brooklyn, Billie. *Sports Car Racing*. New York: PowerKids Press, 2015.

Harrison, Paul. *Extreme Supercars*. London: Arcturus, 2015.

Pipe, Jim. *Fantastically Fast Cars*. Mankato, MN: Smart Apple Media, 2012.

Web Sites

Visit our Web site for links about sports cars:

childsworld.com/links

Note to Parents, Teachers, and Librarians: We routinely verify our Web links to make sure they are safe and active sites. So encourage your readers to check them out!

SELECTED BIBLIOGRAPHY

"Classes." *FIA.com*. World Endurance Championship, n.d. Web. 25 Jun. 2015.

Dedmond, Heather. "What is a GT Car and What Does 'GT' Mean?" *Car Covers Direct*. n.p., 3 May 2013. Web. 25 Jun. 2015.

Spurgeon, Brad. "Le Mans Endurance Race Looks to the Future." *New York Times*. The New York Times Company, 12 Jun. 2014. Web. 25 Jun. 2015.

INDEX

ABOUT THE AUTHOR

Alex Monnig is a freelance journalist from Saint Louis, Missouri, who now lives in Sydney, Australia. He graduated with his master's degree from the University of Missouri in 2010. During his career, he has spent time covering sporting events around the world.